TOP TRUMPS
TANKS

D0255843

© **Haynes Publishing 2007**

All rights reserved. No part of this publication may be reproduced or transmitted in any form or by any means, electronic or mechanical, including photocopying, recording or by any information storage or retrieval system, without permission in writing from Haynes Publishing.

This book is officially licensed by Winning Moves UK Ltd, owners of the Top Trumps registered trademark.

George Forty has asserted his right to be identified as the author of this book.

British Library Cataloguing-in-Publication Data:
A catalogue record for this book is available from the British Library

ISBN 978 1 84425 411 8

Library of Congress catalog card no. 2006936109

Published by Haynes Publishing,
Sparkford, Yeovil, Somerset BA22 7JJ, UK
Tel: +44 (0)1963 442030 Fax: +44 (0)1963 440001
Email: sales@haynes.co.uk
Website: www.haynes.co.uk

Haynes North America, Inc., 861 Lawrence Drive, Newbury Park California 91320, USA

Printed and bound in Great Britain by J. H. Haynes & Co. Ltd, Sparkford

Photographic credits:
Front cover: Challenger 2 © Crown Copyright/MOD. *Reproduced with the permission of the Controller of Her Majesty's Stationery Office.*
Author's collection: 12–15 except 15a (all courtesy General Dynamics Land Systems), 42–43 (courtesy Creusot-Loire), 57 inset, 58, 59a&c, 64–65, 67, 72, 75, 76 and 79a (both courtesy Krauss Maffei), 79a&c (courtesy Krauss Maffei), 89a and 90 and 91b&d (all courtesy Jim R. Osborne), 92, 95b, 100 (courtesy Col David Eshel), 131a, 135a (courtesy Israeli Defence Forces), 140, 143a; Bovington Tank Museum: 8, 16–41, 45 inset, 46, 47a, 52–56, 60–63, 66, 68–71, 74, 77 inset, 78, 80–87, 94, 95c, 98, 99b, 102–103, 106, 108–130, 131b&c, 132–134, 135b&c, 136–139, 142, 143b&c, 144–187; Panzermuseum Munster: 9 (insets), 10–11; Repaircraft plc: 59b; RTR Publications Trust: 44, 47b, 48–49, 51a&b; U.S. Army: 15a, 88, 89b, 91a&c, 95a, 96 and 99c&d (all via Simon Dunstan), 99a&e, 104 (via Simon Dunstan), 105 inset, 107a,b (via Simon Dunstan), 107c; Vickers Defence Systems: 47c, 48 inset, 50, 51c

The Author

Lieutenant Colonel George Forty OBE, FMA served in the British Army for thirty-two years with the Royal Tank Regiment and was formerly the Curator of the Bovington Tank Museum in Dorset. He is the author of over 40 books on military subjects.

TOP TRUMPS

TANKS

Contents

About
Top Trumps

It's now more than 30 years since Britain's kids first caught the Top Trumps craze. The game remained hugely popular until the 1990s, when it slowly drifted into obscurity. Then, in 1999, UK games company Winning Moves discovered it, bought it, dusted it down, gave it a thorough makeover and introduced it to a whole new generation. And so the Top Trumps legend continues.

Nowadays, there are Top Trumps titles for just about everyone, with subjects about animals, cars, ships, aircraft and all the great films and TV shows. Top Trumps is now even more popular than before. In Britain, a pack of Top Trumps is bought every six seconds! And it's not just British children who love the game. Children in Australasia, the Far East, the Middle East, all over Europe and in North America can buy Top Trumps at their local shops.

Today you can even play the game on the internet, interactive DVD, your games console and even your mobile phone.

You've played the game...

Now read the book!

Haynes Publishing and Top Trumps have teamed up to bring you this exciting new Top Trumps book, in which you will find even more pictures, details and statistics.

Top Trumps: Tanks features 45 tanks from around the world, from the very first tank ever built in 1915, through examples from both World Wars, to modern main battle tanks. Packed with fascinating facts, stunning photographs and all the vital statistics, this is the essential pocket guide. And if you're lucky enough to spot any of these tanks, then at the back of the book we've provided space for you to record when and where you saw them.

Look out for other Top Trumps books from Haynes Publishing – even more facts, even more fun!

A7V
Sturmpanzerwagen

A7V
Sturmpanzerwagen

After showing little interest in tanks, the Germans eventually built the A7V Sturmpanzerwagen, 100 being ordered but less than 25 coming into service. Weighing 30 tons, it comprised a boxlike superstructure over a tractor chassis. It had a large crew, twelve of whom were machine gunners. Main armament was a nose-mounted 57mm gun. Cross-country performance was poor, but its road speed was quite high for the period. Despite its frightening appearance it was remarkably ineffective, being both cumbersome and mechanically unreliable. The first tank v tank battle took place on 24 April 1918 – three A7Vs versus two (Female) and one (Male) British Mark IV heavy tanks. After an exchange of fire during which the A7V's armour-piercing machine gun fire penetrated the British tanks, forcing the Females to withdraw, accurate fire from the Male's 6pdr made the A7V take evasive action, during which it ran down a steep bank and overturned.

Entered Service:	1917
Crew:	18
Weight:	30,480kg (30 ton)
Length:	8m (26ft 3in)
Height:	3.4m (11ft 2in)
Width:	3.2m (10ft 6in)
Main armament:	1 x 57mm gun
Secondary:	6 x 7.92mm Maxim-Spandau 08/15 MG
Armour (max):	30mm
Engine:	2 x Daimler-Benz 4-cylinder 100hp, petrol
Speed:	15kph (9mph)
Range:	70km (44 miles)

M1A1/A2 Abrams
Main Battle Tank

M1A1/A2 Abrams
Main Battle Tank

Manufactured by General Dynamics, Abrams is the prime weapon of the US armoured forces. The first M1 came into service in 1978, the M1A1 in 1985 and the M1A2 in 1986. Since then system enhancement packages have ensured it remains one of the most formidable tanks in the world. Built using steel-encased depleted-uranium armour as protection against modern antitank weapons, its main weapon is the 120mm M256 smoothbore developed by Rheinmetall GmbH of Germany. It is crammed full of the most advanced electronic equipment, e.g. the commander's station has independent stabilised day and night vision with a 360-degree view, automatic sector scanning, automatic target cueing of the gunner's sight and backup fire control. The gunner's specially modified seat also locks him in position so that even on the move his eyes are locked in his sight. The Abrams' combat effectiveness has been proved in the recent conflicts in the Gulf, where, together with Challenger, it dominated the battlefield.

Specifications

Entered Service:	1985/86
Crew:	4
Weight:	57,154kg (56.3 ton)
Length:	9.77m (32ft 3in)
Height:	2.44m (8ft)
Width:	3.66m (12ft)
Main armament:	1 x 120mm M256 smoothbore
Secondary:	1 x 7.62mm and 1 x 12.7mm MG
Armour (max):	Not known
Engine:	AGT 1500 gas turbine, 1500hp
Speed:	67kph (42mph)
Range:	465km (289 miles)

A10
Cruiser Tank

A10
Cruiser Tank

Light tanks lacked firepower and medium tanks lacked speed, which led to the design of the 'Cruiser' series, beginning with the A 9 in 1938, and followed by the A 10 two years later. Both had the same designer, hence both had similar features – same basic turret (A 9 was the first British tank with an hydraulically powered turret traverse) and hull shape, but A 10 had no auxiliary machine gun turrets mounted either side of the driver. Extra armour was also added to the A 10, doubling the maximum thickness, by bolting extra plates onto the hull and turret. 175 A 10s were ordered and all completed by September 1940, being first issued to units of 1st Armoured Division. They saw action in France in 1940 and in the Western Desert against the Italians, until late 1941, by which time they were too slow and lightly armoured to confront German tanks of the time.

Specifications

Entered Service:	1940
Crew:	5
Weight:	13,970kg (13.75 ton)
Length:	5.51m (18ft 1in)
Height:	2.59m (8ft 6in)
Width:	2.54m (8ft 4in)
Main armament:	1 x 2pdr gun
Secondary:	2 x 7.92mm Besa MG
Armour (max):	30mm
Engine:	26kph (16.16mph)
Speed:	67kph (42mph)
Range:	161km (100 miles)

A15 Cruiser Mk VI
Crusader Mark III

A15 Cruiser Mk VI
Crusader Mark III

The Crusader was built using many components from the A13 Cruiser series, including both the Christie suspension and Liberty engine, to reduce costs and production time. It had a riveted hull, a welded turret and an extra layer of armour bolted on. The Mark I was ready by March 1940, production was then increased and 5,300 Crusaders (Marks I–III) were produced by 1943. It became the principal British tank until the arrival of the American Sherman. However, Crusader always suffered from unreliability. It first saw action in the Western Desert in June 1941, doing well against Italian armour. Although the Germans respected its speed, it was no match for the Pz Kpfw III or indeed the heavier German anti-tank guns. It was withdrawn from frontline service in May 1942.

Specifications

Entered Service:	1940 (Mk I), 1942 (Mk III)
Crew:	3
Weight:	20,067kg (19.75 ton)
Length:	6.3m (20ft 8in)
Height:	2.24m (7ft 4in)
Width:	2.79m (9ft 2in)
Main armament:	1 x 6pdr gun (Mk III) replacing original 2pdr (Mks I&II)
Secondary:	1 or 2 x 7.92mm Besa MG
Armour (max):	51mm
Engine:	Nuffield Liberty V12, 340hp, petrol
Speed:	44kph (27mph)
Range:	161km (100 miles)

A22 Churchill
Infantry Tank Mk IV

A22 Churchill
Infantry Tank Mk IV

The Churchill was the first British tank to be completely designed during WW2 and was in production throughout the war. The earliest (Mk I) was built in 1941, with a turret-mounted 2pdr gun and a 3in Close-Support howitzer in its nose. With thick armour and a slow but satisfactory cross-country performance, it was one of the most well-liked British tanks of the war. Its size was limited by UK railway loading gauge restrictions, so it was too narrow to take the larger turret needed for the 17pdr gun. Thus by 1944/5 it was seriously under-gunned, although this was partly offset by its thick armour. Churchill was one of the most important British tanks especially because of its adaptability to the specialised-armour roles needed for the invasion of Europe, e.g. flame-throwers, armoured engineer vehicles, various bridge-carriers, mine-clearers and numerous beach landing aids.

Specifications

Entered Service:	1941
Crew:	5
Weight:	39,626kg (39 ton)
Length:	7.44m (24ft 5in)
Height:	3.25m (10ft 8in)
Width:	2.74m (9ft)
Main armament:	1 x 6pdr gun
Secondary:	1 or 2 x 7.92mm Besa MG
Armour (max):	152mm
Engine:	Bedford 12-cylinder, 350hp petrol
Speed:	25kph (15.5mph)
Range:	193km (120 miles)

A27M Cruiser
Mark VIII Cromwell

A27M Cruiser
Mark VIII Cromwell

Early Cromwells resembled their predecessors, apart from the Rolls-Royce Meteor engine (hence the 'M'), which made Cromwell the fastest cruiser tank ever. It also was the most used British cruiser, forming the main tank in 1944–45 armoured divisions, together with the American-built Sherman. Cromwell's hull and turret were of a simple box shape and construction comprised an inner skin with an outer layer of bolted-on armour. A major difference between early and late models was that welding replaced riveting, further simplifying production. There were doubts among some tank crews who converted from Sherman, because it lacked firepower, being armed with a 75mm or 6pdr gun, neither being a match for the Tiger or Panther. Unfortunately Cromwell's narrow hull prevented it being up-gunned until an extensive postwar redesign.

Specifications

Entered Service:	1943
Crew:	5
Weight:	27,941kg (27.5 ton)
Length:	6.35m (20ft 10in)
Height:	2.49m (8ft 2in)
Width:	2.9m ((9ft 6in)
Main armament:	Mks I-III: 1 x 6pdr, Mks IV, V & VII: 75mm, Mks VI&VIII: 95mm howitzer
Secondary:	1 or 2 x 7.92mm Besa MG
Armour (max):	76mm (101mm with added-on armour)
Engine:	Rolls Royce Meteor V12 600hp, petrol
Top Speed:	52kph (32mph)
Range:	278km (173 miles)

A34 Comet
Cruiser Tank

T33522

52   40

A34 Comet
Cruiser Tank

The logical development of the Cromwell design was to produce a
tank that really had the firepower, protection and mobility to match its
German counterparts and this was Comet. All-welded construction and
nearly five tons heavier than the last up-armoured version of Cromwell, it
retained many similar features and components, together with the same
general layout. It was the last British tank to have the Christie suspension
(large road wheels for fast cross-country travel). It had a good cross-
country performance, a top speed of 32mph and mounted a completely
redesigned main gun, a 76.2mm (known as the 77mm). Fast and reliable,
the Comet was the best all-round British tank produced during WW2, but
entered service far too late to have much effect on tank-v-tank combat.
Production began in late 1944, but regiments did not receive them until
after the Rhine crossing in March 1945. It remained in service for the next
fifteen years, its successor being the A41 medium gun Centurion.

Specifications

Entered Service:	1945
Crew:	5
Weight:	35,560kg (35 ton)
Length:	7.66m (25ft 1.5in)
Height:	2.68m (8ft 9.5in)
Width:	3.05m (10ft)
Main armament:	77mm gun
Secondary:	2 x 7.92mm MG
Armour (max):	101mm
Engine:	Rolls Meteor V12 600hp, petrol
Top Speed:	47kph (29mph)
Range:	198km (123 miles)

A41 Centurion
Medium Gun Tank

A41 Centurion
Medium Gun Tank

Centurion was a major British success in design and production. Prototypes were built during WW2, troop trials beginning in May 1945, but it never saw action during the war. Twenty pilot models were ordered, with 17-pounder main guns and a mixture of Polsten cannon or Besa MGs. The Mark II (first production model) incorporated various improvements including a cast turret, commander's vision cupola and a co-axial Besa MG. Over 4,400 Centurions were eventually built, the longest production run (2,800) being the Mark III with such major improvements as a more efficient 650hp Rolls-Royce Meteor engine and a 20pdr main gun with gyroscopic gun control equipment so it could fire accurately on the move. Ammunition was not stored above the turret ring, greatly increasing its survival chances. Many other improvements were made over the years, most importantly the 105mm rifled gun. Centurion saw action in Korea, Vietnam and numerous other wars, having been bought by many nations worldwide.

Specifications

Entered Service:	1945
Crew:	4
Weight:	43,182kg (42.5 ton)
Length:	7.47m (24ft 6in)
Height:	3.02m (9ft 11in)
Width:	3.4m (11ft 2in)
Main armament:	1 x 17pdr, then 20pdr, finally 105mm gun
Secondary:	1 x 7.92mm Besa MG
Armour (max):	101.6mm
Engine:	Meteor V12 650hp, petrol
Top Speed:	35.4kph (22mph)
Range:	193km (120 miles)

AMX 13
Light Tank

AMX 13
Light Tank

Designed just after WWII, the AMX 13 was initially manufactured in 1950 by Atelier de Construction Roanne, then from the early 1960s by Mecanique Creusot-Loire, and finally by GIAT into the late 1980s – a lengthy period that saw it grow into a massive family of successful variants. Its most distinctive feature was the extraordinary rear-mounted, low-profile, oscillating turret. Main armament was initially a long-barrelled 75mm self-loading main gun, then upgraded to 90mm and finally, in 1987, to a 105mm low-recoil gun option. When the AMX 13 was sold abroad some other countries also mounted their own weapons of choice, but all continued with the oscillating turret – which proved to be troublesome. The excellent tough chassis remained essentially the same, though there were changes of engine from petrol to diesel. Regular upgrade packages extended the AMX 13's service life and almost 8,000 vehicles were manufactured in total.

Specifications

Entered Service:	1950
Crew:	3
Weight:	15,000kg (14.8 ton)
Length:	4.88m (16ft)
Height:	2.3m (7ft 6.5in)
Width:	2.51m (8ft 3in)
Main armament:	1 x 75mm, 90mm or 105mm gun
Secondary:	2 x 7.62mm MG
Armour (max):	25mm
Engine:	SOFAM 8-cylinder 250hp, petrol
Top Speed:	60kph (37.3mph)
Range:	400km (250 miles)

Challenger 1
Main Battle Tank

65KG19

Challenger 1
Main Battle Tank

CR1 was based upon an updated variant of Chieftain, known as Shir 1, built originally for the Shah of Iran. CR1 uses advanced Chobham composite armour, together with cast and rolled steel, the emphasis being on protection and firepower rather than mobility. In September 1978, the MOD ordered 243 CR1s from ROF Leeds (later Vickers Defence Systems). Four years later, the Challenger 1 was accepted by the MOD, production being well under way. The first order was sufficient to equip four armoured regiments and in July 1984 there was a further order for 64 more, to equip a fifth. Finally, a further 76 were ordered, the last being delivered in the mid-1990s. Ten years later, the last CR1 was phased out, being replaced by Challenger 2 MBT. During Operation Desert Storm in the first Gulf War, CR1 was heavily involved, destroying some 300 Iraqi MBTs for the loss of no Challengers.

Specifications

Entered service:	1982
Crew:	4
Weight:	62,000kg (61 ton)
Length:	8.33m (26ft 4ins)
Height:	2.5m (8ft 2.5in)
Width:	3.52m (11ft 6.5in)
Main armament:	1 x 120mm L11A5 gun
Secondary:	2 x 7.62mm MG
Armour (max):	not known
Engine:	Rolls-Royce CV 12, 1200hp, diesel
Top Speed:	57kph (35.4mph)
Range:	450km (280 miles)

Challenger 2
Main Battle Tank

Challenger 2
Main Battle Tank

The logical development of the Vickers-built Challenger CR1, was the Challenger CR2. It shares its predecessor's hull and automotive parts, but has many new and improved features, such as its Chobham second-generation composite armour, an NBC (Nuclear, biological and chemical) protection suite, and – for the first time in any British tank – both a heating and a cooling system in the crew compartment! Main armament is a gyrostabilised Royal Ordnance 120mm rifled main gun, the coaxially mounted machine gun being a McDonnell Douglas Helicopter Systems 7.62mm chain gun. Its fire control system is the latest generation in digital computer technology, as are its range-finding, sighting and fire suppression systems. The CR2 was combat-proven in the second Gulf War, and proved to be one of the deadliest current

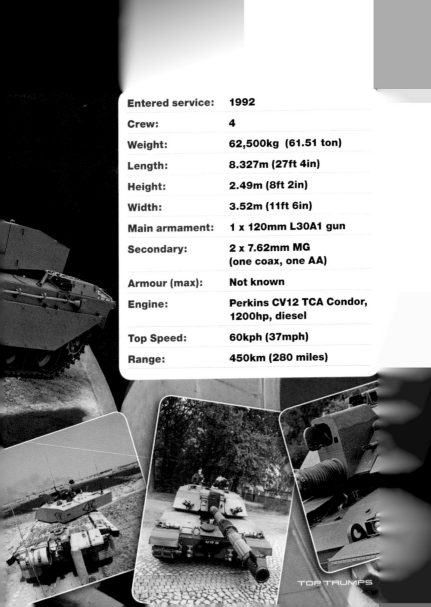

Entered service:	1992
Crew:	4
Weight:	62,500kg (61.51 ton)
Length:	8.327m (27ft 4in)
Height:	2.49m (8ft 2in)
Width:	3.52m (11ft 6in)
Main armament:	1 x 120mm L30A1 gun
Secondary:	2 x 7.62mm MG (one coax, one AA)
Armour (max):	Not known
Engine:	Perkins CV12 TCA Condor, 1200hp, diesel
Top Speed:	60kph (37mph)
Range:	450km (280 miles)

TOP TRUMPS

Char B1-bis
Heavy Tank

Char B1-bis
Heavy Tank

The 'Renault Char de Bataille B1' was built by a consortium of French companies under the code name 'Tracteur 30'. Main armament was a short-barrelled, hull-mounted 75mm gun, sighting and firing being controlled by the driver, who made corrections by turning the tank. Also there was a hull-mounted machine gun fired by the driver, both weapons being loaded by a co-driver. On top was a small turret containing a 37mm gun and another MG, which were fired by the tank commander. The B1-bis (second) version evolved from B1, appearing in 1935. It had thicker armour, a larger gun in the turret and a more powerful engine. Internal traverse was still impossible for the 75mm, so laying and firing was as before. Large numbers of Char B1-bis were captured in good condition by the Germans in 1940.

Specifications

Entered service:	1935
Crew:	4
Weight:	32,500kg (32 ton)
Length:	6.52m (21ft 5in)
Height:	2.79m (9ft 2in)
Width:	2.5m (8ft 2in)
Main armament:	1 x 75mm gun, 1 x 47mm gun
Secondary:	2 x 7.5mm MG
Armour (max):	60mm
Engine:	Renault, 6-cylinder 300hp, petrol
Speed:	28kph (17.4mph)
Range:	180km (111.8 miles)

CVR(T)
Scorpion

366Y

CVR(T)
Scorpion

Built by Alvis as the replacement for the ageing Saladin and Saracen wheeled AFVs, the CVR(T) – 'Combat Vehicle Reconnaissance (Tracked)' – family comprised: Scorpion (fire support); Scimitar (light recce); Spartan (armoured personnel carrier); Samson (recovery); Striker (anti-tank guided weapon); Sultan (command vehicle); and Samaritan (ambulance). All were deliberately compact enough for air transportation. With its light but strong aluminium armour, the Scorpion weighed under 8,000kg, it was fast (50mph), with the same basic design, layout and crew numbers as the Scimitar, but in its turret it mounted a different main gun – the L23A1 76mm, instead of the lighter 30mm Rarden cannon. One of the latest versions of Scorpion is Scorpion 90, which mounts the 90mm Cockerill Mark 3 main gun; another is the Repaircraft plc S 2000 Scorpion Upgrade.

Specifications

Entered service:	1973
Crew:	3
Weight:	7,800kg (7.67 ton)
Length:	4.39m (14ft 5in)
Height:	2.08m (6ft 10in)
Width:	2.18m (7ft 2in)
Main armament:	1 x 76mm or 90mm gun
Secondary:	1 x 7.62mm MG
Armour (max):	Not known
Engine:	4.2 Jaguar 190hp, petrol
Speed:	80.5kph (50mph)
Range:	644km (400 miles)

Renault FT17
Light Tank

Renault FT17
Light Tank

The Char Mitrailleuse (machine gun tank) FT17 was a remarkable little tank, weighing only 6.5 tons. It was the very first tank to have a fully traversing turret, containing a single machine gun. After WW1 the FT17 was copied/adapted/produced by many different countries, including Russia, Japan and America, whilst the French, Americans and British all used them during the war. In British service they were for command and liaison work. A very large number were built and there were seven different models, including one with a cast turret and later a 37mm Puteaux gun replaced the MG. Driving was via a crash gearbox, steering by a clutch and brake system. The first build of 150 commenced in March 1917 and they first saw action on 31 May 1918. Postwar, they formed the basis of many tank armies and some were still in French Army service at the start of WW2.

Specifications

Entered service:	1917
Crew:	2
Weight:	6,604kg (6.5 ton)
Length:	4.09m (13ft 6in)
Height:	2.13m (7ft)
Width:	1.7m (5ft 7in)
Main armament:	1 x 8mm Hotchkiss machine gun
Secondary:	1 x 7.62mm MG
Armour (max):	22mm
Engine:	Renault 4-cylinder, petrol, 35hp
Speed:	7.7kph (4.8mph)
Range:	35km (21.7 miles)

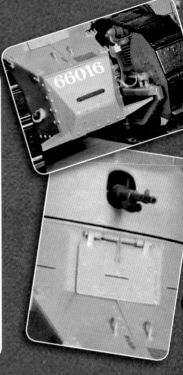

Chieftain
Main Battle Tank

Chieftain
Main Battle Tank

Successor to the world-beating Centurion, Chieftain had early teething problems with its multi-fuel engine (cracking cylinder liners, failure of piston rings, etc). It was also normally run on diesel that was extremely dirty and gave a telltale smoke plume when starting up. Nevertheless, once these difficulties were dealt with it settled down to become a reliable and well-liked tank – the first British MBT. It was of conventional design with the engine, gearbox and transmission at the rear. When closed down the driver reclined, so the overall silhouette was kept as low as possible. Apart from the Mark 1, all subsequent Chieftains were fitted with the fully-integrated Improved Fire Control System, ensuring a high degree of accuracy for its 120mm rifled gun, which used a bagged charge system (projectile and charge loaded separately) – another first on a British tank.

Specifications

Entered service:	**(Mark 1) 1963**
Crew:	**4**
Weight:	**55,000kg (54.13 ton)**
Length:	**7.518m (24ft 8in)**
Height:	**2.9m (9ft 6in)**
Width:	**3.5m (11ft 6in)**
Main armament	**1 x 120mm rifled gun**
Secondary:	**2 x 7.62mm MG (plus 1 x 12.7mm ranging MG, replaced later by a Tank Laser Sight)**
Armour (max):	**Not known**
Engine:	**Leyland L 60 750hp multi-fuel (uprated from 585hp to 720hp, then finally to 750hp)**
Speed:	**48kph (30mph)**
Range:	**4-500km (250–300 miles)**

Leclerc
Main Battle Tank

Leclerc
Main Battle Tank

Developed from an abandoned Franco-German tank design project of the 1980s, the Leclerc entered service in 1992 and is currently the prime weapon of French armoured forces. Built of welded, rolled steel and composite armour, it is fitted with a hydropneumatic suspension system. The main armament is a 120mm smoothbore gun served by an automatic loader. It has the latest digital, optical fire control and battlefield management systems. Future improvements include enhanced command and control systems, battlefield identification (friend-or-foe), automatic target tracking, defensive aids suite, new thermal imager and enhanced armour. A 'stealth' kit is also being evaluated. It is certainly an impressive-looking MBT and should rate highly. However, what it lacks in achieving the 'top gun' status of other MBTs such as Abrams, Challenger 2 and Merkava, is the seal of approval that only combat can give. It has been bought by the United Arab Emirates.

Specifications

Entered service:	1992
Crew:	3
Weight:	56,000kg (55.1 ton)
Length:	9.87m (32ft 4.5in)
Height:	2.53m (8ft 3.5in)
Width:	3.71m (12ft 2in)
Main armament	1 x 120mm smoothbore gun
Secondary:	1 x 12.7mm and 1 x 7.62mm MG
Armour (max):	Not known
Engine:	SACM V8X 12-cylinder, 1500hp diesel
Speed:	72kph (44.7mph)
Range:	450km (280 miles)

Leopard 1
Main Battle Tank

Leopard 1
Main Battle Tank

Originating from an earlier development project shared by Germany, France and Italy, the Leopard 1 was the German tank that resulted when the project failed. Manufactured in 1963 by Krauss-Maffei of Munich, influence from the French AMX 30 kept the armour thin, when compared with other contemporary MBTs, to gain on mobility, although it increased in later Marks. The main armament was the British-made 105mm rifled gun fitted with a gyroscopic stabiliser for accurate firing on the move. The tank was also fitted with automatic fire control, NBC protection and night vision equipment. With its good design and all-round reliability, Leopard 1 has had a successful commercial history – over 6,000 vehicles being exported to nine NATO countries and Australia, as well as being made under licence in Italy. During its lifespan Leopard 1 has seen numerous armour upgrades and variants. Although now replaced by Leopard 2, it is still in service with many other armies.

Specifications

Entered service:	1963
Crew:	4
Weight:	40,400kg (39.76 ton)
Length:	9.54m (31ft 3.5in)
Height:	2.76m (9ft 0.5in)
Width:	3.41m (11ft 2.5in)
Main armament:	1 x 105mm gun
Secondary:	2 x 7.62mm MG
Armour (max):	70mm
Engine:	MTU MB 828 M500 830hp, multi-fuel
Speed:	65kph (40.4mph)
Range:	600km (373 miles)

Leopard 2
Main Battle Tank

Leopard 2
Main Battle Tank

Leopard 2 was also built by Krauss-Maffei, again originating in another failed, shared project, this time between Germany and the USA, known as MBT 70. Utilising many components from that project, Leopard 2 entered service in 1979, after a series of prototypes and intensive trials. This meticulous development cycle has continued with upgrade packages including improved spaced armour, main gun stabilisation, suspension, navigation and fire control systems, and it is still very much one of the leading contemporary MBTs. The main armament was initially the L4, a Rheinmetall 120mm smoothbore, but has more recently been upgraded to the longer barrelled L55, again smoothbore. Used and manufactured under licence by many NATO member countries, Leopard 2 has many variants, mounting different added armour, weapons and fire control systems or modified for specific purposes. The Swiss Army for example, now has some 400 Leopard 2 (Pz 87 Leo) MBTs, largely built in Switzerland.

Specifications

Entered service:	1979
Crew:	4
Weight:	59,700kg (58.8 ton)
Length:	9.97m (32ft 8.5in)
Height:	2.64m (8ft 8in)
Width:	3.74m (12ft 3in)
Main armament	1 x 120mm smoothbore gun
Secondary:	2 x 7.62mm MG
Armour (max):	Not known
Engine:	MTU MB 873 Ka501 12-cylinder, 1500hp diesel
Speed:	72kph (44.75mph)
Range:	500km (310 miles)

No 1 Lincoln Machine

'Little Willie'

No 1 Lincoln Machine

'Little Willie'

The very first tank ever built came into existence in early September 1915. Above its rectangular hull was to be a centrally mounted turret containing a 2pdr gun; however, this was never fitted and instead a dummy was used during the trials. It had British-designed Bullock tracks, brought from America and separate tail wheels (not shown here) towed behind to assist with cross-country performance and steering. It had track problems, having difficulty meeting the War Office requirements – to cross a 4ft wide trench and mount a 2ft vertical step. Then the War Office revised its tests and Little Willie had to be rebuilt to cross a 5ft trench and climb a 4.5ft step. This time the hull was fitted with redesigned tracks and the simulated turret removed. 'Little Willie' (modified) was completed early in December 1915.

Specifications

Entered service:	1915 (prototype only)
Crew:	4 to 6
Weight:	18,290kg (18 ton)
Length:	5.53m (18ft 2in)
Height:	3.05m (10ft 2in)
Width:	2.8m (9ft 4in)
Main armament:	1 x 2pdr gun
Secondary:	1 x 7.7mm Maxim machine gun and up to three Lewis guns
Armour (max):	12mm
Engine:	Daimler 6-cylinder 105hp, petrol
Top Speed:	3.2kph (2mph)
Range:	Not tested

LITTLE WILLIE
-1915-

M3 General Lee/Grant

Medium Tank

M3 General Lee/Grant
Medium Tank

The standard American medium tank of the early war years was the M3, known as the General Lee by the British and armed with a limited traverse 75mm gun in a side sponson, plus a 37mm in a small, fully-rotating turret on top. The British had their own version – known as the General Grant and specially bought under Lend-Lease, which had a number of modifications as a result of battle experience, e.g. no cupola (a ring around the commander's hatch holding vision blocks and hatch lid) giving a lower silhouette, and a larger turret, with room for the radio in a rear bustle, so the radio operator could load the 37mm and coax MG (for the commander). The M3 first saw action with the British Eighth Army in the Western Desert, its 75mm making a significant impact on the Germans. It was, however, soon to be superseded by the M4 medium Sherman.

Specifications

Entered service:	1941
Crew:	6 (7 on Lee)
Weight:	27,219kg (26.7 ton)
Length:	5.64m (18ft 6in)
Height:	3.12m (10ft 3in)
Width:	2.72m (8ft 11in)
Main armament:	1 x 75mm gun
Secondary:	1 x 37mm and 4 x .30in Browning MG
Armour (max):	57mm
Engine:	Continental R 975 radial 340hp petrol
Top Speed:	42kph (26mph)
Range:	193km (120 miles)

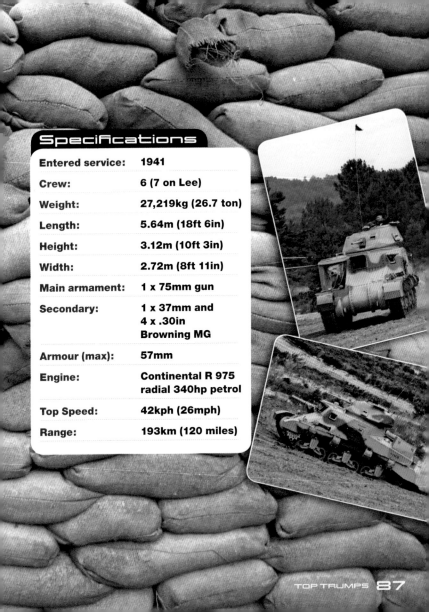

M4 Sherman
Medium Tank

M4 Sherman
Medium Tank

A staggering 49,234 Shermans were built during WW2 – more than half the total tank production of the USA and larger than the *combined* wartime tank output of the UK and Germany! This successor to the M3 Lee/Grant, was the most widely-used Allied tank of the war, its reliability and robustness making it also ideal for adaptation to many different roles as well as gun tank, e.g. amphibians, self-propelled guns, mine clearers, tank destroyers, bridgelayers and so on. As a gun tank, the most powerful of the wartime models was probably the 'Firefly', mounting a British 17pdr gun, and the M4A3 (76), the original M4 having only a 75mm gun. It first saw action with the British Eighth Army in North Africa in October 1942. The Sherman featured here is the M4A1E8 (76) with improved suspension and a 76mm main gun.

Specifications

(mid production)

Entered service:	1941
Crew:	5
Weight:	30,339kg (29.9 ton)
Length:	5.88m (19ft 4in)
Height:	2.74m (9ft)
Width:	2.68m (8ft 10in)
Main armament:	1 x 75mm M3 gun
Secondary:	2 x 7.62mm MG and 1 x 12.7mm AA MG
Armour (max):	75mm
Engine:	Continental R 975 400hp petrol
Speed:	39kph (24.2mph)
Range:	192km (119 miles)

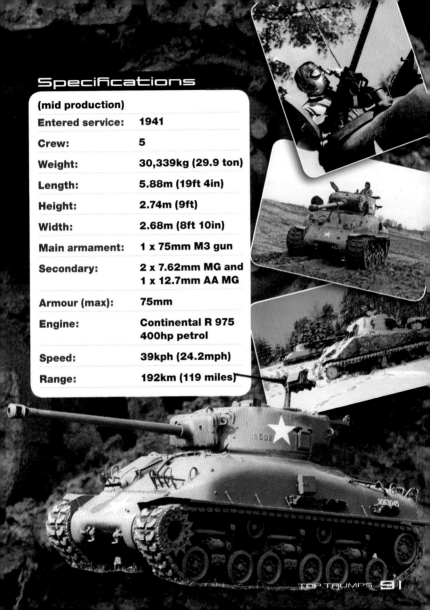

M41 Walker Bulldog

Light Tank

M41 Walker Bulldog
Light Tank

Designed after WW2, the M41 eventually entered service in 1951 after an extensive testing period. The M41 was fast and packed a powerful punch for its size. It saw action in Vietnam and served in many NATO armies, as well as being exported to various countries in South America and Asia, some of whom have carried out extensive modifications as well as building 'look-alikes', e.g. the Brazilian Bernardini M41. Cockerill of Belgium also successfully replaced the 76mm main gun with a 90mm for Uruguay. Thus, although production has long ceased, the Bulldog is still to be found all over the world. Perhaps the strangest use for it was as a remotely controlled target tank for testing missiles! It was also widely used for trial purposes by the USA, especially for work on the M551 Sheridan project .

Specifications

Entered service:	1951
Crew:	4
Weight:	23,495kg (23.1 ton)
Length:	8.21m (26ft 11in)
Height:	2.72m (8ft 11in)
Width:	3.2m (10ft 6in)
Main armament:	1 x 76mm gun
Secondary:	1 x 12.7mm and 1 x 7.62mm MG
Armour (max):	32mm
Engine:	Continental AOS 95-3 500hp, petrol
Top Speed:	72.4kph (45mph)
Range:	161km (100 miles)

M48 Patton
Main Battle Tank

M48 Patton
Main Battle Tank

Rushed into production during the Korean war crisis – and thus initially suffering from teething problems – the M48 went on to have a distinguished, long service life, including combat in Vietnam. With a lower, wider hull and a less bulging turret than the previous M47, it had a powerful searchlight above the main gun. Initially armed with a 90mm gun, it was later upgraded to 105mm. It was one of the first tanks to have an analogue mechanical fire control system and various upgrades had different engines, suspensions, fire control and weapon systems. Very popular on the export market, it was supplied to many countries worldwide, some modifying it for their own specific use, including Spain, Israel and Taiwan (the last being known as 'Brave Tiger' which had an M60 hull, M48 turret, a locally-built 105mm rifled main gun and various fire control and sight gear from the Abrams M1 MBT).

Specifications

Entered service:	1953
Crew:	4
Weight:	48,987kg (48.2 ton)
Length:	9.31m (30ft 6.5in)
Height:	3.01m (9ft 10.5in)
Width:	3.63m (11ft 11in)
Main armament:	1 x 105mm L7 gun
Secondary:	3 x 7.62mm MG
Armour (max):	180mm
Engine:	Continental AVDS 17902 12-cylinder 750hp diesel
Speed:	48kph (30mph)
Range:	496km (310 miles)

M60
Main Battle Tank

M60
Main Battle Tank

M60 is one of the world's most successful MBTs, with over 15,000 built. Since entering US Army service in 1960, it has been sold to over 21 countries. It has had an excellent battlefield record for over 45 years, being continuously upgraded with added-on armour (outside the tank), increasingly powerful engines, new guns and fire control systems, and ammunition. The original main armament was the 105mm M68 rifled gun derived from the British L7A1 105mm gun. The M60A1, built between 1962 and 1980, had a new turret and thicker armour; the M60A2 (built in 1972), had another new turret mounting a 152mm gun and missile launcher. The M60A3 (built 1972–87), had an improved fire control system and was the most successful and numerously built. General Dynamics recently brought out the M60-2000 upgrade package, using the turret and 120mm smoothbore main gun of Abrams, together with a new uprated engine, fire control and safety systems, thus prolonging this excellent MBT's life still further.

Specifications

Entered service:	1960
Crew:	4
Weight:	52,617kg (51.8 ton)
Length:	9.44m (31ft)
Height:	3.27m (10ft 8.5in)
Width:	3.63m (11ft 11in)
Main armament:	1 x 105mm gun
Secondary:	1 x 12.7mm and 1 x 7.62mm MGs
Armour (max):	143mm
Engine:	AVDS 17902A V12 750hp, diesel
Speed:	48kph (30mph)
Range:	500km (311 miles)

M551 Sheridan
Light Tank

U.S. ARMY
12C 77268

M551 Sheridan
Light Tank

The M551 Sheridan is an air-portable American light tank developed in the 1960s for its airborne divisions. Entering service in 1968, the Sheridan's main armament was the MGM-51 Shillelagh tube-launched, wire-guided missile system, which could also fire 152mm conventional ammunition. However, there were many problems with the weapons system, delaying the light tank's entry into service and plaguing it thereafter. Lightly armoured, using aluminium to save on weight, it was vulnerable to a whole range of weapons. In combat in Vietnam the missile system was soon rejected in favour of more conventional munitions, but the Sheridan still did not perform well. Being adversely affected by the moist conditions and with little protection on its hull bottom, it was especially vulnerable to mines. Nevertheless Sheridans continued in service until the 1990s, for example seeing service in the first Gulf War.

Specifications

Entered service:	1968
Crew:	4
Weight:	15,830kg (15.6 ton)
Length:	6.30m (20ft 8in)
Height:	2.95m (9ft 8in)
Width:	2.82m (9ft 3in)
Main armament:	1 x 152mm gun/ missile system
Secondary:	7.62mm MG
Armour (max):	Not known
Engine:	Detroit Diesel 6V53T 6-cylinder 300hp, diesel
Speed:	72kph (45mph)
Range:	600km (373 miles)

Mark I Male
Heavy Tank 'Mother'

Mark I Male
Heavy Tank 'Mother'

Whilst 'Little Willie' was under construction a new tank was being designed with a longer track length, to improve its cross-country performance. This could be achieved with a wheel 6ft in diameter, so the length and shape of track in ground contact had to be as for the lower curve of such a wheel, raising the height of the tank's front, thus producing the now familiar 'rhomboid' shape of British WW1 heavy tanks. Its main armament was mounted in side sponsons to keep the centre of gravity low. 'Mother' passed the War Office tests easily. Building of the first 100 Mark Is began in February 1916, following the same basic design as 'Mother'. Half were Male tanks, half Female (armed with machine guns instead of 6pdrs). The Mark I is recognisable by its tail wheels, the unshortened barrels on its ex-Naval 6pdrs and the chicken wire anti-grenade 'roof'.

Specifications

Entered service:	1916
Crew:	8
Weight:	28,450kg (28 ton)
Length:	9.9m (32ft 6in)
Height:	2.41m (7ft 11in)
Width:	4.19m (13ft 9in)
Main armament:	2 x 6pdr guns
Secondary:	1 x 0.303in Hotchkiss MG
Armour (max):	12mm
Engine:	Daimler 6-cylinder petrol, 150hp
Speed:	5.95kph (3.7mph)
Range:	35.4km (22 miles)

Valentine
Infantry Tank Mk III

Valentine
Infantry Tank Mk III

The prototype was produced on 14 February 1940, hence its name. Over 8,000 Valentines were built in 11 different Marks, with various specialised variants. It remained in production until 1944, being also built under licence in Canada (for the USSR). Valentines accounted for about 25 per cent of British wartime tank production. Over the years construction changed from riveted to welded, and its engine from petrol to diesel – the AEC engines being finally replaced by the more reliable GMC two-stroke diesel. Valentine had various main armaments (see Specifications). Most of its active service was in North Africa, where its range was increased by fitting extra fuel tanks. It was also used by Commonwealth troops in the Pacific and Asian theatres. Variants included a bridgelayer, an amphibian (as seen here), minesweepers, self-propelled guns and a flamethrower.

Specifications

Entered service:	1940
Crew:	3
Weight:	17,272kg (17 ton)
Length:	5.89m (19ft 4in)
Height:	2.29m (7ft 6in)
Width:	2.64m (8ft 8in)
Main armament:	1 x 2pdr, 6pdr or 75mm gun
Secondary:	1 x 7.92mm Besa MG
Armour (max):	65mm
Engine:	AEC 6-cylinder 131hp diesel, or AEC 6-cylinder 135hp petrol, or GMC 135hp diesel
Top Speed:	24kph (14.9mph)
Range:	145km (90 miles)

Mark V
Heavy Tank

Mark V
Heavy Tank

In 1917, British tank design took another major step forward with the **Mark V Heavy Tank**, the first heavy tank that could be driven by one man alone, because it had a four-speed epicyclic gearbox replacing the change-speed gearing of earlier models, which needed a second driver to change gear. The 150hp engine was also specially designed by Ricardo and there were other improvements such as better observation and ventilation, almost double the range of the Mark IV (45 miles instead of 25), 60-gallon armoured fuel tanks fitted at the rear, improved crew escape hatches in the roof and an unditching beam was carried on the hull roof (when bogged it was attached to the tracks by chains, tracks then rotated, bringing the beam down until the tracks could get some grip). 800 Mark Vs were built (400 Male & 400 Female)

Specifications

Entered service:	1918
Crew:	8
Weight:	29,465kg (29 ton)
Length:	8.03m (26ft 4in)
Height:	2.49m (8ft 2in)
Width:	3.91m (12ft 10in)
Main armament:	2 x 6pdr gun
Secondary:	4 x 0.303in Hotchkiss MG
Armour (max):	12mm
Engine:	Ricardo 6-cylinder 150hp, petrol
Speed:	7.4kph (4.6mph)
Range:	72.4km (45 miles)

Mark VI
Light Tank

T4194

Mark VI
Light Tank

The Mark VI was similar to earlier Marks of light tank, but with a redesigned turret to allow room for a radio. There were various versions, the main two being Marks VIA and VIB, a version of the latter being for the Indian Army. The series entered production in 1936 and a thousand were in British service worldwide by the outbreak of World War 2, the little tank thus forming a major part of British tank strength. When the British Expeditionary Force (BEF) sailed for France in 1940, the Mk VI was serving in all divisional cavalry and light tank regiments in 1st Armoured Division. It was widely used in roles other than reconnaissance for which it had been designed, often resulting in heavy losses when pitted against better armed and armoured German tanks. Nevertheless it served with distinction in France, the Western Desert, Greece, Malta, Crete and Syria.

Entered service:	1937
Crew:	2
Weight:	5080kg (5 ton)
Length:	4.01m (13ft 2in)
Height:	2.26m (7ft 5in)
Width:	2.08m (6ft 10m)
Main armament:	1 x heavy MG
Secondary:	1 x light MG
Armour (max):	10mm
Engine:	Meadows 6-cylinder 88hp, petrol
Top Speed:	65kph (35mph)
Range:	209km (124 miles)

Matilda Mk I
A11 Infantry Tank

Matilda Mk I
A11 Infantry Tank

Designed and built in 1936, Matilda Mk1 entered service two years later. Top speed was only 8mph, because it was considered that infantry tanks needed only to keep up with the infantry, who until then had always attacked on foot. In order to keep costs down, its construction was simple with a commercial Ford V8 engine and transmission, while steering controls, brakes, suspension and so on were all adapted from the Vickers light tanks and Dragon gun tractors. It was of mainly riveted construction, with a cast turret. The first production order for just 60 tanks was placed in April 1937, but later increased to 140, all being completed by August 1940. They were soon obsolete – being outgunned from the very start by the German tanks of the day. It is supposed to have been named after a cartoon character because of its duck-like appearance and waddling gait!

Specifications

Entered service:	1938
Crew:	2
Weight:	11,160kg (11 ton)
Length:	4.85m (15ft 11in)
Height:	1.85m (6ft 1in)
Width:	2.29m 7ft 6in)
Main armament:	1 x 0.50in or 0.303in MG
Secondary:	–
Armour (max):	60mm
Engine:	Ford V8 petrol, 70hp
Speed:	13kph (8mph)
Range:	129km (80 miles)

Matilda Mk II
A12 Infantry Tank

Matilda Mk II
A12 Infantry Tank

In 1936, work began on a successor to the Matilda I infantry tank. The new design was based on the A 7 medium and built by the Vulcan Foundry of Warrington. Twin AEC diesel engines and an epicyclic gearbox were installed and the tank was armed with a 2pdr main gun and a coaxially-mounted 7.92mm Besa MG, in a powered turret that could traverse a full 360 degrees in fourteen seconds. Hull armour was cast and the tracks protected by armour side skirts, with five mud chutes. Matilda II played an important role in early Western Desert campaigns, its thick armour being almost immune to Italian tank and anti-tank fire. Until the appearance of the German 88mm gun in 1941/42, it was the most effective British tank. Unfortunately, its turret ring was too small to fit the 6pdr, so its importance then diminished.

Specifications

Entered service:	1939
Crew:	4
Weight:	26,924kg (26.5 ton)
Length:	5.61m (18ft 5in)
Height:	2.52m (8ft 3in)
Width:	2.59m (8ft 6in)
Main armament:	1 x 2pdr gun
Secondary:	1 x 7.92mm Besa MG
Armour (max):	78mm
Engine:	2 x AEC 6-cylinder 87hp, diesels
Top Speed:	13kph (8mph)
Range:	258km (160 miles)

Merkava
Main Battle Tank

Merkava
Main Battle Tank

Merkava (Chariot) is an MBT of innovative design, with special emphasis on crew protection, e.g. the engine is in front, there is extra spaced armour on the frontal arc, side skirts and track protectors, and there are bulkheads between the crew and the fuel/ammunition. There is even a special protective umbrella for the commander when his hatch is open. Another unusual feature are rear doors in the hull, so it can carry extra ammunition or a small squad of infantry.

First appearing in 1979, Merkava 1 mounted a 105mm main gun. Merkava 2 had increased engine performance, whilst Merkava 3 had a new suspension system, a 1200-horsepower engine and new transmission, an upgraded 120mm main gun with a thermal sleeve to increase accuracy by preventing heat distortion and ballistic protection provided by further special add-on armour modules. Merkava 4 has further improved night and remote vision devices, a new MTU 1500hp diesel engine, an enhanced main gun package and increased additional external armour.

Specifications

Mk 3	
Entered service:	1979
Crew:	4
Weight:	62,000kg (61 ton)
Length:	7.6m (24ft 11in)
Height:	2.64m (8ft 8in)
Width:	3.7m (12ft 1.5in)
Main armament:	1 x 120mm gun
Secondary:	3 x 7.62mm MGs
Armour (max):	Not known
Engine:	Teledyne AVDS V12 1200hp, diesel
Speed:	55kph (34mph)
Range:	500km (310 miles)

Panzer Kampfwagen I

Light Tank

Panzer KampFwagen I

Light Tank

The PzKpfw I Ausf A was the first German tank to go into mass production. It had the same hull and suspension as its predecessor, the Pz Kpfw I Ausf A Ohne Aufbau ('without turret') which had been produced without a weapon system because the Versailles Treaty forbade Germany from building tanks. Soon outclassed, it was withdrawn from active service in 1941. The Ausf B had a slightly longer chassis and a more powerful engine, but was also phased out in 1941. Finally, there was a command version (seen here) which was used at all levels in HQs of panzer units from the mid-1930s up to the early war years. The superstructure had to be raised to make room for the radio and its operator. The final model was a 21-ton infantry assault tank, which had very thick armour. Thirty were built in 1942, a few being combat tested in Russia. However, as a result of these tests, further

Specifications

Entered service:	1934
Crew:	2
Weight:	5,893kg (5.8 ton)
Length:	4.42m (14ft 6in)
Height:	1.72m (5ft 8in)
Width:	2.06m (6ft 9in)
Main armament:	2 x 7.92mm MG
Secondary:	–
Armour (max):	13mm
Engine:	Maybach NL38TR, 6-cylinder 100hp, petrol
Speed:	40kph (24.8mph)
Range:	153km (95 miles)

Panzer KampFwagen III

Medium Tank

Panzer KampFwagen III
Medium Tank

The true strength of the Panzer divisions was their medium tanks, first developed in 1935, PzKpfw III being constantly in production from 1937 until 1943, with many versions including variants like flamethrowers, submersibles, command, recovery and ammunition carriers as well as gun tanks. Early models mounted a 37mm gun, plus twin MGs, with a third in the hull. Ausf A entered service in 1937, but was withdrawn in early 1940 because its armour was inadequate. Ausf E mounted the same armament, but had thicker armour. Ausf F (1939) had its turret redesigned for the new 50mm gun. Soon thicker armour and bigger guns were again needed, but the Pzkpfw III turret ring could not accept anything larger than 50mm. 600 Ausf G models were produced from April 1940 onwards, now weighing over 20 tons. Ausf L also mounted a 50mm gun and thicker armour, whilst Ausf M had 'schürzen' (skirts) to protect against close range weapons.

Specifications

Entered service:	1937
Crew:	5
Weight:	19,500kg (19.2 ton)
Length:	5.38m (17ft 4.5in)
Height:	2.45m (8ft)
Width:	2.91m (9ft 10.9in)
Main armament:	1 x 37mm gun
Secondary:	3 x 7.92mm MG
Armour (max):	30mm
Engine:	Maybach V12 300hp, petrol
Top Speed:	40kph (24.8mph)
Range:	165km (102.5 miles)

Panzer Kampfwagen IV

Medium Tank

Panzer KampFwagen IV
Medium Tank

The best German medium tank was Pz Kkpfw IV – the only German battle tank to stay in production throughout WW2, being continually uparmoured and upgunned. It was well made and robust with a good cross-country performance and a large enough turret ring to take more powerful guns. Early models mounted a 75mm low velocity, short-barrelled gun, its role being infantry support. But in 1941 it was decided to improve its firepower by fitting a long-barrelled 75mm gun. The Ausf F was the first to be upgunned, stowage being modified to take the larger rounds. Appearing in mid-1942, it was better than any Allied tanks of the time. More of the Ausf H model were produced than any other German tank. It had better transmission and thicker armour and was the last model but one, the last being the Ausf J, weighing 25 tons, with a range of over 300km and a top speed of 38kph.

Specifications

Ausf F2

Entered service:	1942
Crew:	5
Weight:	22,350kg (22 ton)
Length:	6.63m (21ft 9in)
Height:	2.68m (8ft 9.5in)
Width:	2.88m (9ft 5.5in)
Main armament:	1 x 75mm gun
Secondary:	2 x 7.92mm MG
Armour (max):	50mm
Engine:	Maybach V12 300hp, petrol
Speed:	40kph (24.8mph)
Range:	209km (130 miles)

Panzer KampFwagen VI
AusF E 'Tiger' Heavy Tank

Panzer Kampfwagen VI
AusF E 'Tiger' Heavy Tank

Undoubtedly the most famous of all German tanks was the Tiger, although fewer than 1,400 were ever produced. Tiger production began in July 1942 and it first saw action in Russia in August 1942. Weighing some 56 tons, Tiger's main armament was the converted anti-aircraft/anti-tank gun – the 8.8cm KwK36 L/56 that could penetrate 112mm of armour at 500m, Tiger E being the only vehicle to be armed with this weapon. When it first came into service it could knock out most Allied tanks with ease and soon earned a reputation out of all proportion to its true capabilities. It did have weak points however, one of them being its very slow turret traverse. Tiger E was followed by the even more powerful 68-ton Tiger II or 'Koenigstiger' (bottom right picture), but only 489 were ever built from January 1944 onwards and used in the defensive battles towards the end of the war.

Specifications

Entered service:	1942
Crew:	5
Weight:	56,900kg (56 ton)
Length:	8.45m (27ft 8.5in)
Height:	3m (9ft 10in)
Width:	3.56m (11ft 8in)
Main armament:	1 x 8.8cm KwK 36 gun
Secondary:	2 or 3 x 7.92mm MG
Armour (max):	100mm
Engine:	Maybach V12 , 700hp, petrol
Top Speed:	37kph (23mph)
Range:	195km (121 miles)

Somua S35
Medium Tank

Somua S35
Medium Tank

The SOMUA (standing for 'Societe d'Outillage Mecanique d'Usinage d'Artillerie' who were the builders) was the first tank with all cast construction of both hull and turret, its thick armour providing good protection. Its main armament was an excellent long-barrelled, high-velocity 47mm gun in a one-man turret. Fast and reliable, it was actually better armed and better armoured than many of its German opponents in 1940, but was never available in sufficient numbers, only some 430 of these 20-tonners ever being built. Like all French tanks of the time, they were captured in large numbers by the Germans and then used in their own service (and named PzKpfw 35-S 739(f)). As the tide of World War II turned, some came back once again into (Free) French hands, and they remained in service with the French Army for a considerable time after the war.

Specifications

Entered service:	1935
Crew:	3
Weight:	19,500kg (19.2 ton)
Length:	5.38m (17ft 7.8in)
Height:	2.62m (8ft 7in)
Width:	2.12m (6ft 11in)
Main armament:	1 x 47mm gun
Secondary:	1 x 7.5mm MG
Armour (max):	40mm
Engine:	V8 190hp, petrol
Top Speed:	40.7kph (25.3mph)
Range:	257km (160 miles)

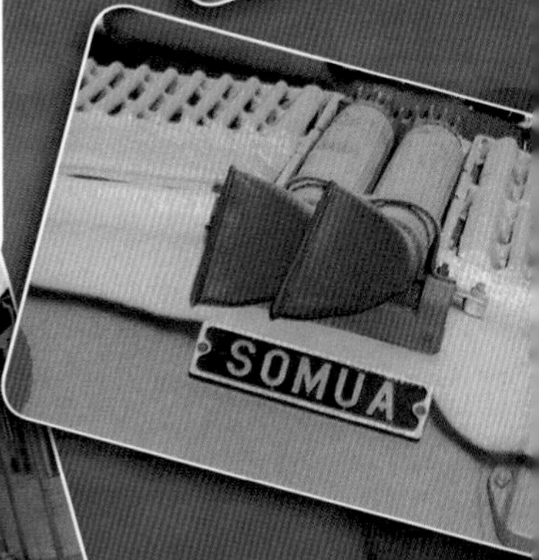

SOMUA

SOMUA

67227

Strv 103 S
Main Battle Tank

Strv 103 S
Main Battle Tank

Highly unusual in design, the S tank, came from a detailed study into hits and injuries sustained by tanks and their crews in combat, showing a high percentage of disabled turrets and guns, with very few impacts below one metre in height. It was therefore decided by the designers to dispense with the turret, mounting the main gun on the chassis, which then had to be turned by the driver to traverse the gun. There was also a front-mounted dozer blade for preparing hull down positions. The main armament was the Royal Ordnance 105mm L7 gun fitted with an automatic loader. 300 Strv 103s were built between 1967 and 1971, equipping three armoured brigades and two independent tank battalions. Removing the traversing turret from any tank undoubtedly reduces its offensive capacity, but conversely increases its defensive capability. This tank design reflects the essentially peaceful, but realistic, intentions of the Swedes.

Specifications

Entered service:	1966
Crew:	3
Weight:	39,700kg (39 ton)
Length:	8.42m (27ft 7in)
Height:	2.50m (8ft 3in)
Width:	3.62m (11ft 10in)
Main armament:	1 x 105mm gun
Secondary:	2 x 7.62mm and 1 x 12.7mm MG
Armour (max):	Not known
Engine:	Rolls Royce K60 490hp, multifuel
Top Speed:	50kph (31mph)
Range:	390km (242 miles)

T34/85
Medium Tank

T34/85
Medium Tank

One of the biggest surprises experienced by the Germans in Russia came some five months after launching Operation 'Barbarossa'. It was a new tank that inflicted heavy losses upon German armour. Armoured expert Gen Guderian was so impressed that he thought the best way to deal with the problem was to copy it! It was, of course, the T34, one of the most important single elements in the eventual Russian victory. Well-armoured, robust and devoid of any frills, it was easily mass produced – another vital factor in its favour. The next in the series, the T34/76D, had a new hexagonal turret, with no overhang as on the previous models. Towards the end of 1943, the T34 became even more lethal by fitting a new 85mm gun in a larger turret. It was claimed that the new gun could penetrate the frontal armour of both Tiger and Panther at 1,000m and

Entered service:	T34/76 – 1940, T34/85 – 1944
Crew:	5
Weight:	32,000kg (31.5 ton)
Length:	8.15m (26ft 7in)
Height:	2.74m (9ft)
Width:	2.99m (9ft 7in)
Main armament:	1 x 85mm gun
Secondary:	2 x 7.62mm MG
Armour (max):	90mm
Engine:	V234 12-cylinder 500hp, diesel
Speed:	55kph (34mph)
Range:	300km (190 miles)

T 62
Main Battle Tank

T 62
Main Battle Tank

T62 was the next development of the T54/T55 series, with an enlarged hull to take a new turret and larger main gun. It became the primary MBT of the Soviet amoured forces during the 1970s. The new centrally located mushroom dome cast turret mounted a U-5T (2A20) Rapira 115mm main gun, with a longer, thinner barrel than the 100mm of T54/55. It also had an automatic shell ejector system, which worked from the recoil, ejecting the spent shell casings through a port in the rear of the turret. A gunner's IR (infra-red) searchlight was mounted on the right, above the main gun. Later models included the usual improvements – gun stabilisation and fire control, NBC, communication and safety systems, add-on armour and increased belly-armour for anti-mine protection. Although there were many variations on the T54/55 chassis, there were surprisingly few on the T62, although the gun tank (over 20,000 built) was upgraded regularly.

Specifications

Entered service:	1961
Crew:	4
Weight:	40,000kg (39.4 ton)
Length:	6.63m (21ft 9in)
Height:	2.39m (7ft 10in))
Width:	3.3m (10ft 10in)
Main armament:	1 x 115mm gun
Secondary:	1 x 7.62mm and 1 x 12.7mm MG
Armour (max):	242mm
Engine:	V55 12-cylinder 580hp diesel
Speed:	50kph (31 mph))
Range:	450km (280 miles)

T 72
Main Battle Tank

T 72
Main Battle Tank

Developed as an alternative to the expensive and highly complicated T64, the classic low rounded turret was centred on the hull with two cupolas – for commander and loader. Main armament was a stabilised 125mm 2A46 smoothbore gun, served by an automatic carousel fitted vertically on the floor and attached to the rear wall of the turret, carrying 28 projectiles. It could fire both the Songster wire guided missile as well as normal munitions. The tank also has a nose-mounted dozer blade to clear obstacles and prepare fire positions, as well as having the usual snorkelling equipment. New versions have many improvements including new engines (850hp then 1250hp), computerised fire control systems, thermal and passive night sights, fire detection and suppression systems. Like others in the series, the T72 was built in massive numbers and supplied to 'client' and satellite states. It was also built under licence by seven other countries including Czechoslovakia, Poland and Yugoslavia.

Specifications

Entered service:	1972
Crew:	3
Weight:	45,500kg (44.8 ton)
Length:	9.53m (31ft 3in)
Height:	2.22m (7ft 3in))
Width:	3.59m (12ft 9in)
Main armament:	1 x 125mm gun
Secondary:	1 x 7.62mm and 1 x 12.7mm MG
Armour (max):	250mm
Engine:	V46 12-cylinder 780hp, diesel
Top Speed:	60kph (37.3mph)
Range:	480km (300 miles)

T 90
Main Battle Tank

T 90
Main Battle Tank

The T90 was developed from the T72BM MBT (the improved version of T72 with built-in reactive armour) and was first manufactured in the late 1980s. It was developed at the same time as T80, but to a less complex and cheaper design. One major difference was in the engine, the T90 being powered by a diesel and the T80 by a gas turbine. It has the classic Russian low, rounded turret with a smoothbore 125mm main gun (as for T72 and T80) firing the AT-11 SNIPER laser-guided anti-tank missile as well as conventional ammunition. T90 has two IR searchlights, one on either side of the gun that are part of its anti-missile defence system. There is also second generation reactive armour on the frontal arc of the turret, so it is one of the best protected of Russian MBTs. It is also equipped with the latest fire control, navigation and safety systems.

Specifications

Entered service:	1993
Crew:	3
Weight:	46,500kg (45.8 ton)
Length:	6.86m (22ft 6in))
Height:	2.23m (7ft 4in)
Width:	3.37m (11ft 1in)
Main armament:	1 x 125mm Rapira 3 gun
Secondary:	1 x 7.62mm and 1 x 12.7mm MG
Armour (max):	Not known
Engine:	V-84MS 12-cylinder 840hp diesel
Top Speed:	60kph (37.3mph)
Range:	500km (310 miles)

Type 59/69
Main Battle Tank

Type 59/69
Main Battle Tank

Both the Chinese Type 59 and its successor, the Type 69, are based on the Soviet T54. Type 59 was the first Chinese tank built under licence and had an identical layout to T54. Initially, it had only the bare essentials, but later models mounted infra-red searchlights, laser rangefinders, night vision equipment and armour enhancements. Both Type 59 and Type 69 have been built in large numbers for the Peoples Liberation Army and for export, and approximately 6,000 are still in service in China. It was sold to over a dozen countries, one of the largest numbers being about 1,200 to Pakistan, which now produces it locally and has exported to other countries in Asia and Africa. The Type 69 was introduced in 1982 and although it looks much like its predecessor it has had a new fire control system, stabilisation, NBC, navigation and safety systems installed. The Type 69-I MBT is now armed with a 100mm smoothbore gun. (The pictures on the previous page, above and middle right show a battle casualty from the First Gulf War.)

Specifications

Entered service:	1980
Crew:	4
Weight:	36,700kg (36.1 ton)
Length:	6.24m (20ft 5.5in)
Height:	2.81m (9ft 2.5in)
Width:	3.3m (10ft 10in)
Main armament:	1 x 100mm smoothbore gun
Secondary:	2 x 7.62mm MG and 1 x 12.7mm AAMG
Armour (max):	100mm
Engine:	1210L-7BW V12 580hp diesel
Top Speed:	50kph (31.1mph)
Range:	420km (261 miles)

Type 74
Main Battle Tank

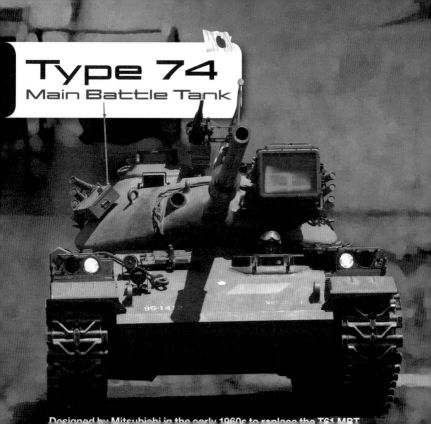

Type 74
Main Battle Tank

Designed by Mitsubishi in the early 1960s to replace the T61 MBT

Specifications

Entered service:	1975
Crew:	4
Weight:	38,000kg (37.4 ton)
Length:	9.42m (30ft 11in)
Height:	2.4m (8ft 1.5in)
Width:	3.18m (10ft 5in)
Main armament:	1 x 105 L7 gun
Secondary:	1 x 7.62mm and 1 x 12.7mm MG
Armour (max):	Not known
Engine:	Mitsubishi 10ZF22 WT 720hp 10-cylinder, diesel
Speed:	60kph (37.3mph)
Range:	440km (249 miles)

Vickers Mk II
Medium Tank

Vickers Mk II
Medium Tank

From 1923, the Vickers Medium Mk I and II were the standard Royal Tank Corps tanks of the interwar years. Both had the same basic chassis, engine, main armament and sprung 'box bogie' suspension, giving the Mk I a top speed of 25–30mph. However, the extra weight – 14 ton instead of 11.7 ton – reduced this for the Mk II to 15mph. Armament comprised a 3pdr, two Vickers MGs in the hull sides and three Hotchkiss around the turret. Externally, the Mk IIs appeared bulkier and the superstructure a little higher. Also, the driver's glacis (sloping front part of the hull) was steeper, the headlights larger and Mk II had suspension skirts. The major mechanical difference was in the steering. In 1932, modifications were made, resulting in the Marks II* and II**. A total of 160 Medium IIs were built but were obsolete before WW2, being under-armoured and suffering from a short track life.

Specifications

Entered service:	1925
Crew:	5
Weight:	14,224kg (14 ton)
Length:	5.33m (17ft 6in)
Height:	2.69m (8ft 10in)
Width:	2.79m (9ft 2in)
Main armament:	1 x 3pdr
Secondary:	3 x 0.303 Vickers MG
Armour (max):	12mm
Engine:	Armstrong-Siddley 8-cylinder 90hp, petrol
Top Speed:	24kph (15mph)
Range:	193km (120 miles)

Checklist

A7V
Sturmpanzerwagen
Date   **Location**

M1A1/A2 Abrams
Main Battle Tank
Date   **Location**

A10
Cruiser Tank
Date   **Location**

A15 Cruiser Mk VI
Crusader Mk III
Date   **Location**

A22 Churchill
Infantry Tank Mk IV
Date   **Location**

A27M Cruiser
Mk VIII Cromwell
Date   **Location**

A34 Comet
Cruiser Tank
Date   **Location**

A41 Centurion
Medium Gun Tank
Date   **Location**

AMX 13
Light Tank
Date   **Location**

Challenger 1
Main Battle Tank
Date   **Location**

Challenger 2
Main Battle Tank
Date   **Location**

Char B1-bis
Heavy Tank
Date   **Location**

CVR(T)
Scorpion
Date   **Location**

Renault FT17
Light Tank
Date   **Location**

Chieftain
Main Battle Tank
Date   **Location**

Leclerc
Main Battle Tank
Date   **Location**

Leopard 1
Main Battle Tank
Date   **Location**

Leopard 2
Main Battle Tank
Date   **Location**

No 1 Lincoln Machine
'Little Willie'
Date   **Location**

M3 General Lee/Grant
Medium Tank
Date   **Location**

M4 Sherman
Medium Tank
Date   **Location**

M41 Walker Bulldog
Light Tank
Date **Location**

M48 Patton
Main Battle Tank
Date **Location**

M60
Main Battle Tank
Date **Location**

M551 Sheridan
Light Tank
Date **Location**

Mark 1 Male
Heavy Tank 'Mother'
Date **Location**

Valentine
Infantry Tank Mk III
Date **Location**

Mark V
Heavy Tank
Date **Location**

Mark VI
Light Tank
Date **Location**

Matilda Mk I
A11 Infantry Tank
Date **Location**

Matilda Mk II
A12 Infantry Tank
Date **Location**

Merkava
Main Battle Tank
Date **Location**

Panzer KampFwagen I
Light Tank
Date **Location**